What God begins in the beginning,
He brings full circle in the end

The Magnificent Story

Julie-Allyson Ieron

What's in between holds
one awe-inspiring plan

ISBN 978-1-945818-05-9

Contact the author at www.joymediaservices.com

Published by Joy Media Publishing, Mt. Prospect, IL

Scripture quotations unless otherwise indicated are taken from the New American Standard Bible, © 1960, 1962, 1963, 1968, 1971, 1972, 1973, 1975, 1977, and 1995 the Lockman Foundation, La Habra, Calif. Used by Permission.

All cover and interior art in the public domain, sourced from Pixabay.com. The publisher and author wish to thank the artists of Pixabay for their great generosity in sharing their talents freely.

Design by Julie-Allyson Ieron for Joy Media Publishing

To you, dear reader

What began as a class project for The Story of Scripture course at Dallas Theological Seminary has grown into this book and its companion live presentation.

My prayer is that, as you read, you will be enthralled by the grandeur of God's magnificent plan that began before time, spans all of human history, and continues throughout eternity. It is one unified story, conceived by the Almighty Creator God, and it holds a role for every soul who ever lived.

I pray you may find your place in this magnificent story and live it out for the rest of your days.

Blessings and prayers, Julie

With thanks to our beloved congregation
at Central Baptist Village
and to chaplain Mike Weber,
who offered a willing audience
for the first public presentation of
The Magnificent Story.

What God begins in the beginning,
He brings full circle in the end.

What's in between holds
one awe-inspiring plan.

Stay tuned for added study opportunities:

95: Key Elements of the Story and
Where to Find Them

101: Study Questions for
Personal, Group and Family Discovery

And now the scene opens on …

The Magnificent Story

In the beginning ...

    In the beginning ... God

        In the beginning God ... ***created***

In the beginning God created ...
    Everything.
        Everything!

And it was good.
    So good. ...
        So good.

In the beginning God created ... Adam
 In the beginning God created ... Eve
And it was *very* good. **VERY** good.
In the beginning God placed
 Adam and Eve in Eden
And there was joy
 And there was communion
 And there was work
 valuable work;
 energizing work.
And it was good. So good. ***So good.***

Unapproachable glory
Unattainable majesty
Inconceivable holiness
Hovered o'er the deep.
Spoke a Word and the world appeared
Separated the skies from seas,
Molded clay and the earth was filled
Breathed a breath—man came alive!

Fill this temple with your magnificence
Fill the hollow in this place
With Your presence O Lord
Unworthy though it is
You have chosen to come in
Fill this temple, fill this place
Creator Omnipotent

The garden was full of life
and of beautiful fruits of all kinds.
There was one tree, only one,
that the Creator placed off limits.

Eat of them all, He told Adam.
Just not *that one.*
For if you eat it, you will die.
In the beginning ...

But all was not well in
    the perfect garden.
Paradise was too soon
    invaded by a
    subtle enemy;
As his body twisted and slithered,
    so his words did the same.
He challenged Eve to question
    the motives and intentions
      of her loving Creator.

"Did God really say?"
And he expelled from his throat
    a sinister laugh.

Eve tried to answer him
     but as she spoke,
          she began to doubt everything.
So she examined the forbidden fruit
     and saw how lovely it was.

And she ate.
     And she gave to Adam
          who was with her.

In that moment what was good
was now tainted.
This seemingly small act of rebellion
Brought death
and deterioration
and division.

Between God and mankind,
between man and woman,
between the creation
and its loving Creator.

And yet ...

In the beginning God ...

Before He created anything
     God had a master plan

In that plan, He prepared a way

For His creation to be restored
          in majestic glory,
               back to paradise,
                    back to fellowship,
                         back to ... *HIM!*

14

"And you, serpent,
            be certain of this:

The seed of the woman
      will one day arise.
You will bruise His heel,
      But He will *crush your head.*"

The plan was in place,
      The players were set.
            The Magnificent Story was afoot.

Unbelievable choice man made
Indescribable arrogance
Inconceivable consequence
Communion was destroyed
The Creator unveiled a plan
He would save them, becoming Man
Choose a woman to mother Him
Redemption was begun.

Fill this temple with your magnificence
Fill the hollow in my heart
With Your presence O Lord
Unworthy though I am
You have chosen to come in
Fill this temple, fill my heart
Creator Omnipotent

17

So the first family's fall didn't
    take the Creator by surprise.

While His perfection couldn't abide their sin,
    His love for the beings
        He brought to life
    Wouldn't let Him leave them in
        their hopeless state.
His master plan began to play out
    as the days and years unfolded.

Smaller stories wove in and out of the plan,
as human history marched forward.

But always …
The Magnificent Story progressed
through the generations.

And always it was … ***unstoppable.***

The fall had its consequences—
    just as the Creator had warned.
Evicted from the garden.
    Introduced to pain.
Enmeshed in interpersonal controversy.
    Separated by sin
        from their Holy Creator.

And then Death entered the scene—
just as the Creator had warned.
Death brought on by
jealousy,
disobedience,
and hatred.

Brother killed brother.
And grief,
unspeakable grief ,
accosted the first family.

21

Sin wasn't satisfied alone.
　　　It multiplied like greedy flames.
Until the Creator determined
　　　to wipe out the entire earth
　　　　　to cleanse it.

Still, His heart loved.
　　　Still His heart yearned
　　　　　to be compassionate
　　　　　　　to the small pinnacles
　　　　　　　　　of His creation.

So He called a man named Noah.

And gave him a task.

According to the Creator's blueprint,

Noah spent a lifetime building an ark.

When the time came,

Creator God locked Noah and

his family in the ark,

with paired representatives

of every animal

on earth.

The rains came,

forty days and forty nights.

and purged the earth.

Finally, finally, the waters receded
　　and the Noah family
　　　　emerged from the ark of safety.

It took virtually no time back on land
for Noah and his son to sin
for all to see.

The purge had proven incomplete.
Sin was too insidious.
The grip of death and destruction
was too powerful.

Could no one rescue mankind?

As people multiplied once again,
the human race showed
its heart of darkness.
"Let us build a tower
to make our name great
and reach to the heavens!"
So they tried.

But at Babel, their purpose failed.
God foiled their lofty plan.
He scattered them abroad.
He splintered their language.

More suspicion and division,
discord and hatred followed.

Nevertheless, God had given His word:

One born of woman
would restore what was lost.

He is always true to His word.

For that reason, and that reason alone ...

The Magnificent Story remained

unstoppable.

Enter Abram, in the land of Ur.
        Abram and his wife Sarai.
God chose him and made him a promise
More than a promise,
        a covenant,
                a guarantee,
                        no strings attached.

"I will call you Abraham and your wife Sarah;
        You are father of a multitude of nations
                She is mother of nations."

He promised Abraham ...
>A people
>>A land
>>>A worldwide blessing

But Abraham and Sarah remained childless.
What of the promise of God?
>Should they take matters
>>into their own hands?

That proved problematic
>with the birth of Ishmael,
>>son of Abraham
>>>and Sarah's servant Hagar.

Waiting for God to move proved
    ever more challenging
Yet, in God's perfect time,
    When Abraham was 100
        and Sarah 90 ... yes, *90!*

Isaac was born.
    Child of God's
        inconceivable promise.

God tested Abraham
"Sacrifice your promised son to Me."

With grieved heart,
        Abraham stood at the altar,
                Ready to obey.
                        Sword poised over the boy.

At the last moment,
God stopped his arm from falling
        and provided a ram
        for the sacrifice.
Abraham's faith in God
        was counted
                righteousness.

33

Isaac grew and fathered twins,
     Esau and Jacob by his wife Rebekah.
Jacob God loved;
     but Esau forfeited his birthright.
No hero in his conduct,
Jacob, deceiver and conniver,
     was deceived into taking two wives.
Sisters Rachael and Leah became
     mothers of Jacob's sons and daughter,
       they and their maids.

Jacob favored Joseph, Rachael's older son,
which made the boy's brothers,
like Cain generations before,
seethe with *hate*.

The brothers threw him in a pit
and sold him into slavery.
They told their father
he was killed by wild beasts.

Joseph conducted himself rightly
    in the land where he was taken,
And God was with him,
    even in his slavery.

He rose to prominence once ...
Was falsely accused
    and imprisoned ...
Then was promptly forgotten.

But God never forgets.

In a moment God elevated Joseph
    to second in command in all Egypt.
When his unsuspecting brothers
    traveled to Egypt
            to beg to purchase food,
    It was Joseph they found in charge.

Yet he forgave,
            and brought their father
                    and their families to safety.

God renewed His promise to Jacob:
"I will call you Israel,
I will be your God."
On his deathbed, Israel spoke to his sons.
Leah's third son, Judah,
received his first
and most powerful
prophetic blessing.
His descendent would hold the scepter—
the ruler's staff.

Generations came and went
    until a Pharoah arose in Egypt
        Who had never heard of Joseph.
Israel's small family had become
    great in number
        and Pharoah feared them.
So he enslaved them
    and worked them harshly,
Until they called out to God to save them.

God heard their cries.

He raised up Moses to declare to Pharoah:

"Let My People Go!"

Through agonies
   and plagues,
        God worked on their behalf.

Still Pharoah wouldn't budge.

"Let My People Go!"

One last plague ... was the harshest of all.
The death angel took the lives of
all the firstborn males of Egypt,
But passed over the households
of Jacob's descendants
who sacrificed a lamb and
spread its blood
on their doorposts.
A spotless lamb's blood
protected Israel's children.
So God delivered His people.

At this, Pharoah finally agreed to
let them go ...
then he had second thoughts.
He pursued them to the edge of the sea.

Just then, God parted the sea,
    and Moses led God's people to safety
        on dry ground.
But Pharoah and his armies
    were swallowed up in rushing waters,
        never to be heard from again.

Then Miriam, Moses' sister, led the women
    and Moses led the people
        in a song of victory.

Sing to the LORD,
    for he is highly exalted.
Both horse and driver
    he has hurled into the sea.
The LORD is my strength and my defense;
    he has become my salvation. Exodus 15:1-2

It didn't take long for the people
    to doubt their miracle-working God.
In the wilderness they saw Him
    as a cloud by day
        and a pillar of fire by night.
    O to have seen Him!

They tasted the heavenly manna.
    O to have tasted!

They drank water from the rock.
    O to have sipped from this stream.

Yet they doubted.
    Fussed and fumed.
        Mumbled and grumbled
            and complained.

God called Moses up the mountain
To give the law
　　to govern the promised land.
And God made a covenant with Moses
　　to take to the people.

And Moses remembered
God's unconditional
covenant with Abraham:

A people
A land
A worldwide blessing.

With this new covenant,
    there were strings
      attached:

If the people obey, they
    will have abundance.
If the people disobey,
    they will suffer consequences:
      Hunger
        Strife
          Displacement from the
            land of promise.

This time there were sacrifices to be made
    Bloody, gory sacrifices
      to cover over sin,
        to remind them that
          someone had to die
            to pay their debt.

Before Moses could come down
    from the mountain,
        the people were already sinning
            by worshipping a golden calf.
In fury, Moses broke the tablets
    written by God's finger,
        as the people broke the law.

Punishments came.

A second time God wrote the law.

This time, when Moses presented
    God's covenant,
        the people gave their word:
They would comply with the law—
    desiring the blessings,
        understanding the consequences
          of disobeying.

Not many days later,
Moses sent twelve to spy the land
       God was giving them.
The spies were conflicted
While Joshua and Caleb told the people
       to trust the God of Moses,
The people believed the ten spies
       who gave a fearsome account.

Since they refused to go forward
God sent them on another lap
       around the desert. A long lap!
For forty years they wandered.

When the new generation
    of wanderers grew
And the first generation perished—
    except Joshua and Caleb—
        it was time to take the land.
New spies went in.
A harlot named Rahab,
    a foreigner, a Jericho-ite,
Believed God would
    give His people the land.
Where His own people had doubted,
    Rahab believed.
        She protected the spies.
So, when the walls of Jericho fell,
    the spies brought Rahab
        and her family to safety.

And Rahab married Salmon
      of Caleb's family,
From the house of Judah—
      of whom the blessing had been spoken
Of a scepter and an eternal crown.

God ruled the people
    in the land of promise
By the covenant He had laid out.
When the people obeyed, they prospered;
When they disobeyed,
    They suffered famine and war.

As in days of Egypt,
    they would call out in their distress
As in days of Egypt,
    God would hear and answer.
For He always hears a repentant heart
    that calls to Him for rescue.

And so He would raise up judges
    to restore the land and the people
      to it.

Until they failed and
    sinned again.

In these days during famine,
A man of Judah
took his family to forbidden land.
There he died.
His two sons, after marrying foreigners,
also died.
Leaving their mother
and two widowed Moabite women
alone.

The women heard there was bread
in Bethlehem.
One daughter-in-law stayed behind.
Yet Naomi and Ruth returned
to the House of Bread.

Ruth took her mother-in-law's
    customs,
        traditions,
           and God.
And God honored her.

Again she married
    into Judah's promised line.

This time she bore a son.

That son bore a son,
    and he after him.

And that grandson of Ruth
    became Israel's greatest king:
        David.

Yet before God elevated David
    to the throne,
The people chose their *own king:*
    Saul.
        Handsome.
          Tall.

Kingly in appearance ... but not in heart.

He started well,
    but his grievous sin
        brought a great downfall.

Julie-Allyson Ieron

David was God's choice,
A man after God's heart
Who though sinful—
    knew how to repent.
After sinning with
    Uriah's wife,
        he sought and
            found God's forgiveness.
King and poet,
David wrote his prayers to God
Creating songs of
    praise,
        petition,
            and repentance.

David received God's third covenant:

    "I will establish your legacy
        A son from your line
            will rule your kingdom
                before Me *forever.*"

After David came Solomon.
He prayed for wisdom
      and gave common sense insights
          through his proverbs of truth.
Solomon built a magnificent temple
      to the Lord His God.

These kings united the realm,
      expanded its influence,
          honored the God of their fathers.

Until Solomon's heart turned away
      from God to worship idols
          brought into his palace
              by forbidden foreign wives.

After Solomon, the kingdom divided.
>Israel and Judah.
>>Ten tribes to the north
>>>Two to the south.
As the kings' hearts went,
>so did the people.

Israel's kings sinned. All of them did evil.
Although prophets Elijah and Elisha
>called them to repentance,
The covenant breaking was great
>and the kingdom of Israel fell.
Its people were carried away to Assyria.
>**Enslaved.**

59

Still in the land of promise,
Judah had a few good kings
    who led the people back to God.
These heeded prophets like Isaiah
    and priests who held to God's law.

But they dotted the landscape
    amid otherwise wicked kings.

In the end, covenant breaking led
    Judah into captivity in Babylon.

What of the promises?
What of God's covenants with Abraham
     and Moses and David?
There was now no king.
       No kingly line.
            No land.
                 How could there be a
                      worldwide blessing?

**Was this the premature end
of The Magnificent Story?**

61

Hear the prophet Jeremiah to the people of Judah as they trudged off to Babylon:

> "Behold, days are coming,"
>   declares the Lord,
> "when I will make **_a new covenant_**
>   with the house of Israel
>   and with the house of Judah."
>   Jeremiah 31:31

And again, through Jeremiah
    God promised captivity
        wouldn't be permanent.

After seventy years,
    He would punish Babylon
        and bring His people home.

God's word proved true.

A remnant of His people
    returned to the land
        just as promised ...

After seventy long, miserable years
    in bondage.

Over more than a century,
    under many leaders,
        against much opposition,
God's people rebuilt the temple,
    restored the broken walls
        re-established their presence
           in the land of promise.

Governor Zerubbabel
    and Joshua the priest,
Organizer Nehemiah
    and Ezra the Scribe,
        helped reset the people's hearts
          toward worship of the
            One, true God.

They saw to it that the chronicles
    and the covenants were read.
Psalms of praise and prayer were sung.
God's law again became law of the land.

Still no king from the tribe of Judah
    sat on David's throne.

After the last three prophets wrote:
    Haggai,
        Zechariah,
            Malachi

God ... was ... silent.

God was silent ...
>   for four centuries.

But don't ever mistake His silence
>   for His apathy
>   or His inactivity.

The Magnificent Story *was still afoot.*

Throughout the silent years
    God was at work:

    Preparing roads,
    Raising kings and kingdoms,
    Establishing languages
        and communications,
    Readying His people of promise
        in the land

Until the moment was right.

Remember again
    those magnificent covenants.

To Abraham God promised
    a people
        a land
            a worldwide blessing

To Moses God promised
    a land flowing with milk and honey
        if the people would obey His law.

To David God promised a son
a Messiah
a King to rule
on his throne forever.

To Jeremiah God promised
a *New Covenant*
written on their hearts,
Where God would dwell
with His people forever.

The Magnificent Story demanded
    a magnificent birth.
When the moment came
    God sent the angel Gabriel
        to a village called Nazareth,
    To Mary, of the house
        of Judah and David,
    Promised in marriage to Joseph,
        also of Judah's kingly line.

Announcing the seed of the woman
    would be born,

Son of Mary ...
    Son of Almighty Creator God

And so, in the line of David
With ancestors who included
    Abraham ... Isaac ... and Jacob
And Rahab formerly of Jericho
And Ruth formerly of Moab
And Bathsheba—
    formerly the wife of Uriah,
        against whom King David
           sinned greatly.

Into this family,
    God in human flesh was born—
        Jesus Christ, Son of God!
           Immanuel, God with us.

For more than three decades,
Jesus lived right with us.
Walked dusty roads.
Toiled and labored.
Bound Himself to the world
He created.
Spoke His Father's eternal truth
to all who would listen.

He came to His own people,
but most received Him not.
Still, to all who did receive Him,
to those who believed in Him ...
To them He gave the right
to become children of God.
John 1:14

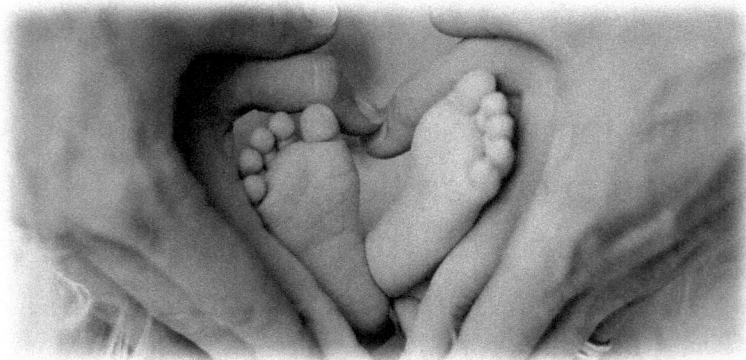

The men and women who followed Jesus
    had many questions.
They often misunderstood His plans.
They saw all of His miracles,
    yet they doubted
        and feared
           and wavered.

Still they stayed near Him,
    because in Him they found
        the words of eternal life.

And then one day,
The rebellion of the serpent of Eden
        took its best shot
                at the Seed of the Woman.

In jealousy and hatred
        that old serpent
                sprung at the Christ.
Its venom loaded
        with all its seething poison,
And then ...
        its fangs tore into the flesh
                of the King of Kings.

And He was nailed to a cross.
And He died.

It wasn't for Himself that He died.
He never sinned. Not ever.
But because we each sinned
and deserved death,
He died in our place,
shed His blood
to pay our debt.

*The perfect Son of God
exchanged His life for ours.*

Was this the end of *The Magnificent Story?*
How could it be?
Not the end.
In fact it was the plan all along.
Since before creation itself.

As promised back in Genesis,
the Seed of the Woman
would crush the serpent's head.
Yes, He laid down His life for us ...
But it was His to take up again.

After three days, Jesus picked up His life
     from His Father's hand,
and He rose victoriously from the grave.

Not just that, but He lives.
     Still today and forevermore, He lives.

Just as His ministry team
    was ready to see Him
        take the Kingdom,
They watched Jesus lifted into the clouds.

Yet again, the Maker of Heaven and Earth
    shocked them.

As the clouds swallowed their Lord,
Beside them stood two gleaming men,
    announcing,

    Stop looking up, you have work to do.
    This same Jesus you saw go up
    will come back the same way.

Days later they were equipped and filled
    by the Holy Spirit He sent in His place.
They were now ready to follow His directive
    to become His witnesses
To Jerusalem ...
    To Judea and Samaria ...
        To the uttermost parts of the earth.

It wasn't always easy to know
His will
His plans
His guidance
Once He had ascended back to Heaven.

Even with the Holy Spirit,
the growing group of followers
didn't always know
how to conduct themselves
as His people.

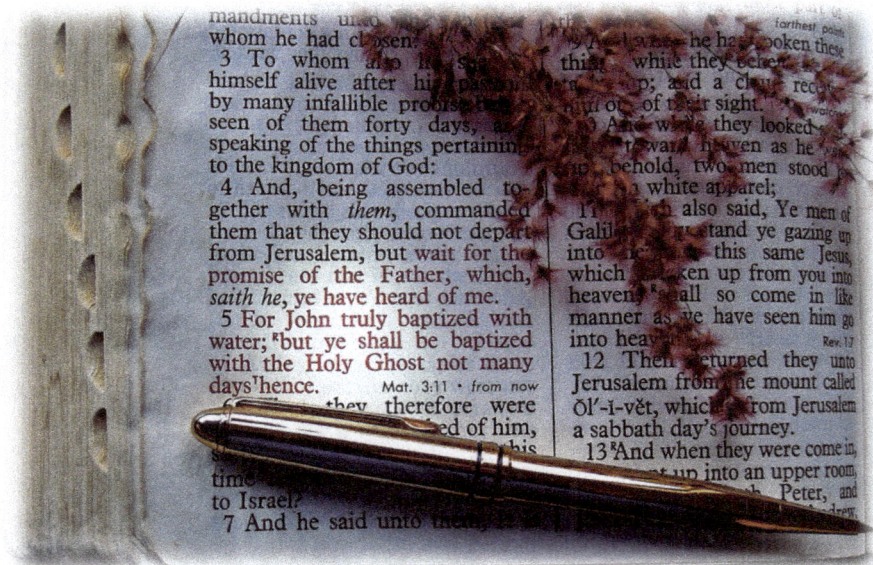

But His remaining disciples
    and those who joined them,
        including the former
            persecutor named Paul,
                taught them well.

They left written legacy in the Gospels
    and letters we call the Epistles.
The Gospels tell the life of Christ.
The Epistles explain and encourage and
    prompt followers to godliness.

Unbelievable choice I have
Indescribable joy it brings
Inconceivable price He paid
Communion to restore
The Creator has died for me
Through His sacrifice pardoned me
Holy dwelling creates in me
If I invite Him in.

Fill this temple with your magnificence
Fill the hollow in my heart
with Your presence O Lord
Unworthy though I am
You have chosen to come in
Fill this temple, fill my heart
Creator Omnipotent

Wait! Notice this:
>   there's a key bit of covenant
>   left to fulfill.

There's not yet a seat
>   for Christ the Messiah
>   on the Throne of David
Not on this earth … Not yet.

No Magnificent Story—
>   no self-respecting story of any kind—
Has a beginning, a middle,
>   and no end.

This story's ending is yet to come.

We know much about the ending.
But not everything.
Most of what we know comes from
what the Exalted Christ revealed
to John on the Isle of Patmos.
And from scenes described by prophets
like Daniel and Ezekiel
back in the Divided Kingdom
and exile days.

Here's what matters ...
Here's what we know for absolute certain:
God keeps His word
He never makes a promise
He will not keep.

So what has He promised?

He will come to receive His people
And one day soon,
        Jesus will reign
                on David's throne
                        on earth!

He will eradicate evil
and put that serpent
where he belongs forever.

King Jesus will dwell among us.
And He will be our light.
And He will be our God.
And He will write His law
on our hearts.

And we will be His people.
Forever!
For always!
For eternity!

The last book, Revelation,
        fulfills all that began in Genesis.
                It brings the whole story full circle.

One scene in Revelation 5
        is especially telling,
                because one day
                        we'll all be in that scene—
                                if we've trusted Jesus.

Imagine, just imagine,
        what that day will be like ...

Then I looked, and I heard the voices of many angels around the throne and the living creatures and the elders; and the number of them was myriads of myriads, and thousands of thousands, saying with a loud voice,

> "Worthy is the Lamb that was slaughtered to receive power, wealth, wisdom, might, honor, glory, and blessing."

And I heard every created thing which is in heaven, or on the earth, or under the earth, or on the sea, and all the things in them, saying,

> "To Him who sits on the throne and to the Lamb *be* the blessing, the honor, the glory, and the dominion forever and ever."

And so *The Magnificent Story* takes us
From the Garden of Eden
    to the Holy City
        come down out of heaven
           to be our eternal home.

And God's Messiah reigns forever and ever
    On the throne of His father David.

And we reign with Him
    His chosen, purchased
        from every tribe and tongue
            by His precious blood.

And that's only the beginning
    of a brand new story,

More magnificent than the first.

Holy, holy, holy
All the saints adore Thee
Casting down their golden crowns
Around the glassy sea

Cherubim and seraphim
Falling down before Thee
Which wert and art
And evermore shalt be

Holy, holy, holy
Lord God Almighty
All Thy works shall praise Thy name
In earth and sky and sea.

Holy, holy, holy
Merciful and mighty.
God in three persons
Blessed Trinity.

"Holy, Holy, Holy"
Reginald Heber, 1783-1826

Lord Jesus, we pray we will live our roles
    in *The Magnificent Story*
        until we see Your face

For today, our best response,
    our only possible response
        to this *Magnificent Story*
Is to accept the salvation You purchased
    by shedding Your blood for us.
And to worship You now and forever,
    in wonder, awe, and praise!

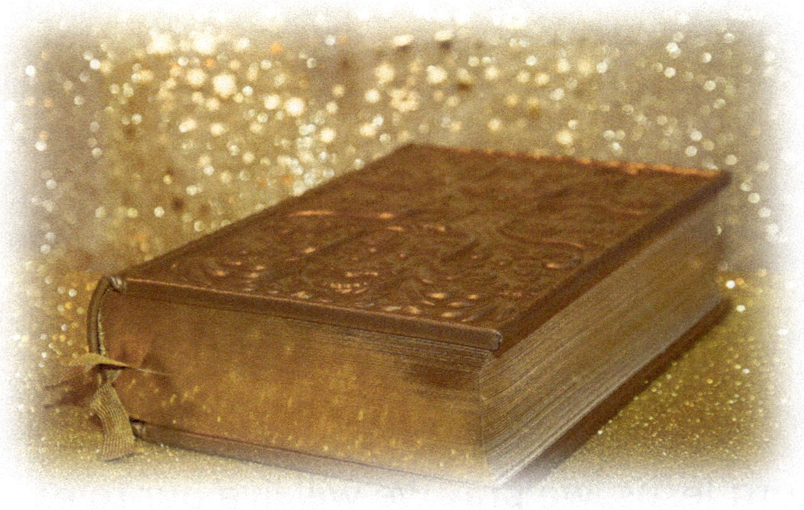

Key Elements of the Story and Where to Find Them

Old Covenant
(Old Testament: Genesis—Malachi)

Genesis 1-2 .... Creation

Genesis 3 .... Entrance of sin

Genesis 6-9 .... Flood

Genesis 12:1-3, Genesis 15, 17....... God's Covenant (promise) with Abraham

Genesis 21-38 .... Isaac, Jacob, Joseph

Genesis 39-50 .... Into Egypt

Exodus 1-15 .... Out of Egypt

Exodus 34:19-28 .... God's Covenant with the people of Israel

Exodus 13 ff, Leviticus,
Numbers, Deuteronomy .... Israel in the Desert

Joshua, Judges, Ruth, 1 Samuel...... Israel in the Promised Land

2 Samuel, Kings, Chronicles .... The United Kingdom

2 Samuel 7 .... God's Covenant with David

1 Kings 12 ff, 2 Chronicles 10 ff ...... The Divided Kingdoms

1 Kings 17 ff,
Isaiah—Zephaniah .... Prophets Warn of Consequences

2 Kings 17 .... Samaria Taken Captive to Assyria

2 Kings 25, 2 Chronicles 36:13........ Judah Taken Captive to Babylon

Ezra, Nehemiah,
Haggai, Zechariah, Malachi .... Remnant of Judah Returns to the Land

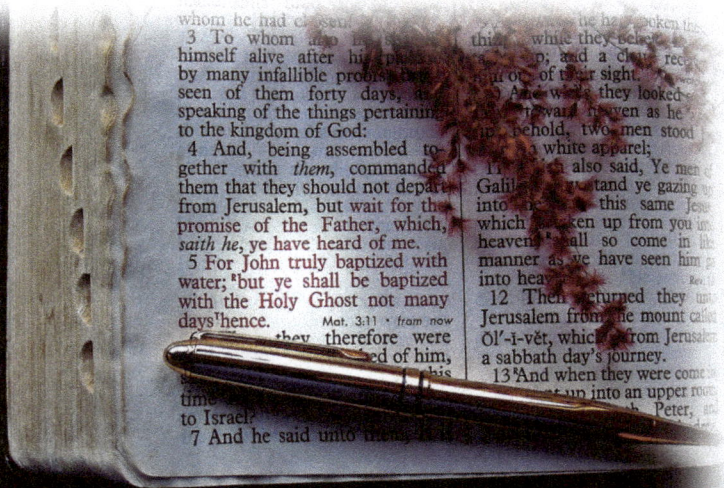

New Covenant
(New Testament: Matthew—Revelation)

Luke 1-2, Matthew 1-2 .... The Birth of Christ

Matthew, Mark, Luke, John .... The Life and Teachings of Christ

Matthew 27, Mark 15,
Luke 23, John 19 .... The Death of Christ

Matthew 28, Mark 16,
Luke 24, John 20 .... The Resurrection of Christ

Acts .... The Birth of the Church

Acts 2 .... The Holy Spirit Is Poured Out

Romans—Jude .... The Letters to the Churches

Revelation .... The End and the New Beginning

Divisions and Stylistic Content of the Bible Books

Old Testament

Beginnings (Books of Moses)

Genesis, Exodus, Leviticus, Numbers, Deuteronomy

History (Birth and Life of a Nation)

Joshua, Judges, Ruth, 1&2 Samuel, 1&2 Kings, 1&2 Chronicles, Ezra Nehemiah, Esther

Poetry and Wisdom Literature

Job, Psalms, Proverbs, Ecclesiastes, Song of Solomon

Prophecy

Isaiah, Jeremiah, Lamentations, Ezekiel, Daniel, Hosea, Joel, Amos, Obadiah Jonah, Micah, Nahum, Habakkuk, Zephaniah, Haggai, Zechariah, Malachi

New Testament

Gospels (Life of Christ Jesus)

Matthew, Mark, Luke, John

History (Birth of the Church)

Acts

Letters to the Churches and Believers

Romans, 1&2 Corinthians, Galatians, Ephesians, Philippians, Colossians 1&2 Thessalonians, 1&2 Timothy, Titus, Philemon, Hebrews, James 1&2 Peter, 1,2&3 John, Jude

Prophecy

Revelation

Study Questions
For Personal, Group, and Family Discovery
Beginnings

1. Why does the writer of Genesis open the entire story of God's interaction with humanity with such a powerful declaration of God's hand at work in the created order of the universe? If He is indeed Creator, how does that impact His authority over it all? Over humanity? Over our individual lives?

2. Consider the contrast between the pre-sin Garden of Eden and life from the moment of disobedience onward to today. How did sin change the human experience on planet Earth? Why was one little act of impertinence such a major deal to God? Why couldn't people just apologize and make everything good again?

3. What is the impact of knowing that sin's entrance into the Garden, and because of it into each of us, didn't take God by surprise? What evidence is there in Genesis 3 that God knew all along and had a plan already in process at the moment of creation—way before the fall?

4. What does it mean that God will use the seed of the woman to crush the serpent's head? (Genesis 3:15).

5. How does God's interaction with Adam and Eve, as well as with others like Noah and Abraham, demonstrate His love for individual people He created? What does this mean to you, personally?

Chosen by God

1. Considering the clear evidence that Abraham, Sarah and their descendants were far from perfect in their faith or actions, why do you think God chose to use them in His plan? Why did God make an unconditional covenant with Abraham? Why is it significant that this covenant didn't hinge on what Abraham did or didn't do?

2. How do the lives of Jacob and his son Joseph clearly demonstrate God's personal intervention? What forces were working against these patriarchs? Why was God so involved in protecting, guiding, and directing them along His planned path? Again, how does this observation impact your journey with God?

3. When the family of Jacob (Israel) grew and became a nation of millions, how did God's interactions with them change? How did He provide for this new people group? How did the enemy of God use Pharoah and others to try to derail God's plan for His people?

Growing into a Holy Nation

1. Read Leviticus 20:26. What did it mean to the people of the Old Testament nation of Israel that they were called by God and separated out (the definition of holiness) for His service? Knowing what you do about the call of Jesus on His disciples, consider what it means to you to be called by God to be His servant. Read 1 Peter 1:16 and 1 Thessalonians 4:7 for hints.

2. How did God preserve His people through their wilderness wanderings? Look for specific examples in the book of Exodus, and in the books of Deuteronomy and Joshua.

3. How did God's leading of His people change when they took possession of the land He promised to them? (See Exodus 13:21-22 and compare it with the calling of the Judge Othniel in Judges 3:9-10, and with the closing line of Judges: 21:25).

4. Read 1 Samuel 3:1. Why was the word of the Lord rare in these days? How did that change when God raised Samuel as both judge and prophet? Now read 1 Samuel 8:6-7. Why did the people reject God as their king? Consider how this pained both Samuel and God Himself.

5. Compare the kingly reigns of Saul, David, and Solomon. What did each

accomplish? What weaknesses did each have? What do you learn about God's grace from observing each king's life story?

Two Nations, Not So Holy

1. Why did the kingdom of Israel divide after Solomon's death? (Find clues in 1 Kings 12.) How did prophets Elijah and Elisha try to call the Northern Kingdom back to the God of their fathers? Why did the kings and the people fail to return? What pull did their worship of false gods have on them? Why did that kingdom fall to invaders first?

2. What impact did a few good kings have on the Southern Kingdom (Judah)? Consider Uzziah in 2 Chronicles 26, Hezekiah in 2 Chronicles 29-30 and Josiah in 2 Chronicles 34-35. What did these kings have in common? What actions did they take? What weaknesses did they have?

3. What happened to the people when good kings led them? What does this mean to modern-day people and those in authority over us? Read 1 Kings 19:18, which was written about the Northern Kingdom. How can people stay true to their God even when evil seems to be ruling and reigning?

4. Why did Judah eventually fall to the Babylonians? Read 2 Chronicles 36:15-16 for clues. Then read vv. 22-23 to see how God worked to call His people back after their time of suffering for their disobedience was over.

5. Every time it looked like evil had derailed God's plan for good, God surprised everyone and rescued His people again. What does that mean for us when we fail and finally come back to Him with repentant hearts?

When All Seems Lost

1. Read Isaiah 53. Discuss the many references to the promised Messiah and how He would suffer and bear the sins of mankind. Consider this

from the perspective of knowing how Jesus lived and died. Then consider that Isaiah's prophecy came hundreds of years before Christ's advent.

2. Why do you suppose God revealed so much to Isaiah in advance? How does this impact your confidence that His plan for you will never be thwarted?

3. What was God orchestrating during the 400 years between the Old Testament and the New Testament? Consider key historical events of that time period including the rise of Alexander the Great and the spread of the Roman Empire. How did those events impact the coming life of Christ the promised One and the eventual spread of the church throughout the known world?

A New, Living Way

1. As the New Testament (another way to state the new covenant promised to Jeremiah in Jeremiah 31:31-33) opens, what is the significance of the virgin birth of Jesus? How does this harken back to Genesis 3?

2. Search the four Gospels to learn all you can about the sinless life of Jesus as He walked this planet as a man. How did He treat others? How did their plights impact Him? How did He relate to genuine seekers? How did He relate differently to the religious elite who challenged His authority? What authority did He have? (See Matthew 28:18.)

3. Why is it so significant that Jesus led a sinless life? (See 2 Corinthians 5:21.) Why is it also significant that Jesus relates to every struggle we face? (See Hebrews 4:15.)

4. When Jesus hung on the cross, how were the prophecies of Isaiah 53 fulfilled? Stop and thank God for the cross and for what it means to your eternal future and your life today.

5. What difference does the empty tomb and Jesus' resurrection make for the believer in Him? Why is it hard for many to believe in this miraculous event? What proof is there of the resurrection? (If you have questions,

check out Lee Strobel's thought-provoking books including, *The Case for Christ, The Case for Easter* and *The Case for a Creator*.)

God Builds His Church

1. How did the disciples change from cowering, fearful deserters to power-ful, convincing witnesses of the risen Christ? What new power source equipped them? (See Romans 8:11 for a clue). Also, read Acts 2 to see the transformation as it happened.

2. If God's Holy Spirit's indwelling power can do that for these men and women, what can He do within you?

3. What is your role in God's growing kingdom? How are you helping ad-vance His message? What difference does His story make on how you go about your daily life? How does Jesus' commission impact you? (See Matthew 28:19-20.)

The End Is the Beginning

1. List some of the ways God has fulfilled promises related to covenants He made with His people. What does this tell you about whether He will be trustworthy and faithful to you? What does this tell you about His ability to fulfill the remainder of His covenant promises?

2. Why does it help to know the end of *The Magnificent Story?* Or, as one popular contemporary Christian song calls it: "The End of the Beginning"? As we encounter obstacles, much like those the early church faced (persecution, unbelief, a contrary world ...), what difference does it make to realize the ultimate victory is yet to come?

3. Read 1 Corinthians 10:13. Then read Revelation 2:7. How will you over-come the challenges of your life? In Whose power? With what amazing promise?

4. Why does the Tree of Life that appears first in Genesis 3 show up again in heaven, as described in Revelation 2:7? What reassurance—even joy— does this offer to you today?

Making His Story, Your Story

1. Have you trusted what Jesus did on the cross to make a way for you to participate in the victory of *The Magnificent Story?* If you have, sing a song of worship and praise to Him for the awe-inspiring eternal gift He has purchased for you.

2. If you haven't yet trusted Him for your eternal destiny, please consider doing that today. Here is a brief prayer you might voice to God—your Creator—to ask Him to apply Jesus' sacrifice to your sin account:

Dear Father in Heaven,

I come to You only because of Jesus, and I use His name to enter Your holy presence.

I know I have broken Your law, I have sinned. And I know there is no way I can make things right or do enough good things to fix what my sins have broken.

I now see that Jesus' death on the cross opened the only way for me to be saved from the death penalty I am owed because of my sins.

So, I ask You to forgive me because of what Jesus did on that cross.

I repent—I am sorry for my sins and I turn my back on them.

Please give me Your Holy Spirit to live in me and make me Your child. I invite Him to empower me to live the rest of my life to honor You.

Thank You, Lord Jesus for saving me right now.

Amen.

If you prayed the prayer to receive Christ or if we can assist you in knowing more about *The Magnificent Story* and about committing your life to Jesus Christ, please write to the author at j-a@joymediaservices.com.

If you would like to check Julie's availability to present this story live and in person to your group or gathering, write to her booking agent Joy at conferences@joymediaservices.com.

To learn more about Julie's ministry and her dozens of books, devotionals, and Bible studies, visit our website at:

joymediaservices.com